Original title:
Yonder Myths Along the Griffin Tusk

Author: Johan Kirsipuu
ISBN HARDBACK: 978-1-80562-071-6
ISBN PAPERBACK: 978-1-80563-592-5

A Pilgrimage Through Celestial Gardens

In gardens where the starlight gleams,
The flowers whisper ancient dreams,
Each petal holds a secret bright,
Beneath the cloak of silken night.

The moonlight dances on the streams,
Illuminating silver beams,
The air is sweet with mystic lore,
Inviting souls to wander more.

With every step, the shadows play,
Leading the heart where spirits sway,
In fragrant paths of endless hope,
As wonders weave and visions scope.

The breeze unfolds its gentle song,
Where fleeting moments still belong,
Each sigh of night, a gentle kiss,
A wandering soul finds fleeting bliss.

The stars above begin to twirl,
A cosmic dance, a wondrous whirl,
In gardens lush, love intertwines,
In this celestial realm, it shines.

The Twilight Saga of Winged Guardians

Beneath the veil of twilight's gleam,
The guardians watch, as shadows teem,
With wings outspread against the dusk,
Their hearts hold secrets, strong and husk.

With gentle grace, they soar on high,
Embracing dreams that kiss the sky,
Each feathered stroke, a tale unfolds,
Of whispered courage and of bolds.

In twilight's glow, the horizons flare,
As ancient myths entwine the air,
Their eyes aglow with sparks of light,
The guardians dance through eternal night.

Through battles fought in silent grace,
They weave through shadows, find their place,
Each flutter holds the strength of hearts,
In every beat, a world departs.

The twilight calls, and they shall rise,
To guard the dreams beneath the skies,
In every flight, a spark ignites,
The saga lives in endless nights.

The Dreamer's Flight Beyond

In twilight's grasp, the whispers soar,
Where shadows dance on moonlit floor.
With hearts aflame, we chase the night,
To realms where dreams take fearless flight.

Beyond the clouds, our spirits climb,
In search of treasures lost in time.
The stars will guide, the winds will sing,
A symphony of hopes takes wing.

Elysian Wings Above the Horizon

Above the hills where soft winds blow,
Elysian wings in golden glow.
With laughter light, they weave and glide,
Through painted skies, our dreams abide.

Each dawn unfolds a magic tale,
Where courage blooms and fears grow pale.
Together we will face the morn,
With every breath, our spirits reborn.

Chronicles from the Echoing Abyss

In caves where echoes softly dwell,
Ancient whispers weave a spell.
Each word a treasure, lost yet found,
In shadows deep, where secrets abound.

The lantern flickers, truths arise,
Through dusty pages, time defies.
We walk the path of those who've passed,
In stories held, forever cast.

Stories Woven in Starlight

In the tapestry of night so bright,
Stories woven pure in starlight.
Each spark a voice, each twinkle a tale,
Of love and loss, of winds that sail.

Beneath the vast celestial dome,
We find our hearts, we find our home.
With every wish upon the sky,
Our dreams take root, forever fly.

A Journey Through the Beak of Dawn

When night surrenders to soft light,
The world awakens, dreams take flight.
With whispers of dawn, we softly tread,
Through silver mist where hopes are bred.

A golden brush paints the waking skies,
As birds take wing with joyful cries.
We follow the path where legends lie,
Beneath the gaze of a watchful eye.

A river sparkles, glistening bright,
Reflecting the promise of endless height.
The melody of morning fills the air,
Guiding our steps with a tender care.

Each heartbeat echoes, a steady drum,
In the heart of dawn, a tale begun.
As shadows fade and dreams dissolve,
In the embrace of day, we resolve.

Through fields of gold and forests deep,
The journey calls, igniting our leap.
In the beak of dawn, our spirits rise,
To chase the stars across clear skies.

Legends of Fire and Feather

In realms where whispers weave their tales,
Majestic beings take to the gales.
With wings of flame and hearts of grace,
Fire and feather, in fierce embrace.

At twilight's edge, the stories soar,
Of phoenix flight to a distant shore.
In every flicker, a spark ignites,
Legends born of unyielding nights.

They dance above in a blazing swirl,
As ancient secrets begin to unfurl.
In every ember, a hero's name,
Unyielding flames, yet never the same.

Oceans of stars, the sky's vast gown,
Woven with threads of gold and brown.
In the echo of their vibrant song,
Stirs the spirit to where we belong.

Through trials faced with fire's embrace,
And feathers soft, in fierce grace.
We write our truth, we forge our fate,
In legends' light, we resonate.

The Lost Chronicles of the Skyward

Beneath the arch of endless blue,
Where whispers drift and dreams come true.
The chronicles wait, lost yet near,
In the skyward tales we hold most dear.

With pages worn by time's gentle hand,
In each chapter, a mystic land.
Where giants roam with wise old eyes,
And secrets dwell beyond the skies.

Through storms and calm, the stories flow,
Of gallant hearts and the seeds they sow.
With every turn, the past ignites,
Illuminating lost starlit nights.

A map of dreams unfolds its grace,
As we wander through time and space.
In every story, a voice will guide,
As we seek the truths that worlds provide.

The skyward beckons with a quiet start,
In whispers woven, a beating heart.
The lost chronicles call us to see,
The wonders hidden in you and me.

In the Shadow of Mythic Beasts

In shadows deep, where secrets creep,
Mythic beasts in silence sleep.
With eyes aglow and wisdom vast,
They guard the tales of ages past.

From mighty roars to whispers soft,
In caverns dark, their dreams take off.
With scales of emerald, wings of gold,
Their stories woven, a tapestry bold.

Through forest dense and mountains high,
Lurks the promise beneath the sky.
A dragon's heart, a griffon's grace,
In the magic of moons, we find our place.

As twilight descends, their legends rise,
A tribute sung to the starry skies.
In every shadow, a flicker glows,
Of grandeur lost as night bestows.

In tales of old, we write our part,
With ink and quill, we bare our heart.
In the shadow of beasts, let courage dwell,
For within their sighs lies our own spell.

Riddles of the Indigo Sky

In twilight's grasp, the secrets weave,
A tapestry of stars so strange,
Each shimmer holds a whispered plea,
A mystery that wants to change.

What shadows dance on midnight's breath,
What tales do lanterns softly tell?
Where dreams and wishes lurk in depths,
Beneath the cosmic, vibrant spell.

The indigo stretches wide and far,
A canvas painted by the night,
What riddles hide in every star?
What truths in darkness seek the light?

Echoes bounce from heart to heart,
Each pulse a code, a silent rhyme,
In every search, we play our part,
A dance through space and endless time.

So gaze upon the endless sea,
Of cosmic wonders yet to find,
Embrace the night, the whispered glee,
For in these skies, our fate entwined.

The Unveiling of the Celestial Crest

Upon the hill where shadows lie,
A beacon glows with ancient grace,
Illuminating secrets high,
The crest of stars, a hidden place.

With every breath, the air feels thick,
A pulse of magic in the night,
Where time stands still, and dreams grow quick,
A realm where darkness yields to light.

The whispers from the cosmos call,
Inviting souls to join the quest,
To journey where the ancients fall,
To seek the truth in every crest.

What legends wait in moonlit haze?
What visions chase the fleeting cloud?
In stillness, magic forms and sways,
Awakening hearts, fierce and proud.

So join the dance of night and day,
Embrace the wonders yet untold,
For in this realm, we find our way,
As stars reveal their hearts of gold.

Mysteries on the Edge of the World

On cliffs that kiss the roaring sea,
Whispers curl in the salty air,
Each wave a secret, wild and free,
A tale of wonders, harsh yet rare.

What myths are cast in shadows deep?
What dreams are lost in ocean's sweep?
The edge awaits, a brink of fate,
Where time collapses, spirits wait.

With every gust, the past returns,
An echo of forgotten might,
The fire of history softly burns,
In twilight's glow, a spark ignites.

Beneath the stars, the world stands still,
Inviting seekers to explore,
The mysteries that hearts may fill,
At the precipice of evermore.

So stand upon that ancient stone,
And feel the weight of yesteryears,
For in this place, all paths are known,
The edge of worlds, a cradle of tears.

The Last Soar of Myth and Stone

When twilight sings its gentle tune,
And shadows dance on hallowed ground,
The tales of old begin to bloom,
In whispers where lost dreams are found.

What legends tread on mottled paths?
What creatures linger in the mist?
The echoes of their ancient laughs,
A memory that longs to exist.

Beneath the arch of twilight's glow,
The myths arise, in flight they soar,
Chasing the dusk, the ebb and flow,
Of time entwined with tales of yore.

In every stone, a heartbeat lies,
Each fragment holds a glimpse of fate,
As stars begin their nightly rise,
Soars the heart, the dream awaits.

So cast your eyes upon the skies,
And listen to the stories told,
For in the last, the spirit flies,
In timeless realms, forever bold.

Legends of the Ethereal Guide

In the heart of a misty glade,
Whispers of tales linger and fade.
A guide draped in silken night,
Seeking souls with gentle light.

With each step the shadows sigh,
Echoing dreams that never die.
Faint glimmers dance in the air,
Tales of love beyond compare.

Through ancient woods and silver streams,
Hope arises, woven in dreams.
Hearts entwined in nature's hold,
A story of courage, yet untold.

In the stillness, echoes call,
Of bravery that won't let fall.
Ethereal wisdom guides the way,
As night replaces the light of day.

So gather 'round, let the lore unfold,
Of heroes, mysterious and bold.
In every whisper, magic thrives,
In the legends where the spirit lives.

The Golden Echo of the Dawn

As dawn breaks on the waking world,
The tapestry of light unfurled.
Golden hues paint the sky so bright,
Chasing away the remnants of night.

Voices of morning softly sing,
To the promise that day will bring.
A symphony of warmth and cheer,
In every heartbeat, the world is clear.

Birds take flight on wings of fire,
Filling the air with sweet desire.
Each note a wish for what's to come,
Under the spell of the morning drum.

Fields of dew glisten like jewels,
Nature awakes, breaking all rules.
Dancing petals in the breeze,
Whispers of sunlight through the trees.

In every moment, magic stirs,
Binding tales where life occurs.
The golden echo calls us near,
A reminder that hope is here.

Parables Under a Dappled Sky

Beneath a sky, so soft and bright,
Where whispers of wisdom take their flight.
A canvas painted with dreams anew,
In shades of green and vibrant blue.

Each leaf, a story waiting to share,
Dreams carried on the gentle air.
Dappled shadows play on the ground,
In each heartbeat, lessons abound.

For the world is woven in threads of fate,
Where each encounter holds a gate.
From the smallest seed to mighty trees,
A tapestry spun by nature's pleas.

Moments sparkle like dew at dawn,
In the quiet, a new hope is drawn.
Under the branches, we find our way,
In parables spoken, hearts learn to stay.

As dusk approaches, the stories blend,
A journey begun, a world to mend.
In every sigh, a chance to grow,
Under the sky's radiant glow.

Odes to the Forgotten Beasts

In shadows deep where legends keep,
Forgotten beasts in silence leap.
With fur like dusk and eyes like stars,
Guardians clad in ancient scars.

Through overgrown paths, their spirits roam,
Whispering tales of a long-lost home.
The thunderous roar of the heart's true core,
Echoes of magic forevermore.

From phoenix grace to dragon's might,
Creatures of wonder take to flight.
In the twilight hush, their stories unfold,
In every heartbeat, their courage bold.

Yet in the shadows, some hearts may ache,
For paths forgotten, and the bonds we make.
Embrace the whispers the forest holds,
In every story, a truth unfolds.

So raise your voice to the sky above,
In honor of those we've come to love.
Odes to the beasts who shaped the land,
In memory's embrace, we take our stand.

The Siren's Flight Over Distant Dreams

Upon the waves where shadows play,
The sirens sing both night and day.
Their melodies both sweet and bold,
Awake the dreams that must be told.

From distant shores they lure the lost,
With whispered words, no matter the cost.
Their haunting calls break through the night,
Entwined in magic, they take flight.

The vessels drift, drawn by the sound,
Where secrets of the ocean abound.
In every note, both pain and glee,
The sirens weave their tapestry.

Each sailor hopes to find the way,
To dreams that shine like stars in gray.
Yet many drown 'neath sea's embrace,
For sirens hold a deadly grace.

In quiet moments, hearts will sigh,
As echoes linger, never die.
For those who hear the sirens' plea,
Shall face the depths, forever free.

Guardians of the Lost Horizon

Beneath the skies of dusk's soft hue,
The guardians wait, both strong and true.
Amidst the whispers of the trees,
They guard the dreams like ancient keys.

With watchful eyes, they scan the land,
To weave the fates by heart and hand.
Each star that glimmers through the night,
Guides weary souls to find their light.

When shadows dance, and fears arise,
The guardians rise to silent cries.
With gentle strength, they banish dread,
And light the path where dreams are bred.

Their stories told in legends old,
Of courage found in hearts so bold.
Though time may pass, their watch remains,
As hope's sweet song within us reigns.

So if you wander, lost in thought,
Remember that you're not forgot.
For somewhere near, their presence glows,
The guardians guide where wisdom flows.

The Starlit Path of the Mythical

On starlit paths where whispers tread,
The mythical rise, the lost are led.
With creatures born of lore and dream,
They light the way with a silver beam.

Through forests deep and mountains high,
Underneath the vast and twinkling sky.
The legends walk with those who seek,
In every shadow, they'll softly speak.

A dance of light, a flicker here,
The mythical, both far and near.
With stories wrapped in every star,
They remind us who we really are.

Each step we take on this sacred ground,
Is woven with tales that shall abound.
So lift your gaze and clear your mind,
For all you seek, the stars will find.

In every heart, there lies a spark,
An echo deep, a glowing mark.
For on the path where legends dwell,
The magic lives, and all is well.

Beneath the Roost of the Celestial

Beneath the roost of stars divine,
Where dreams alight and fates entwine.
The whispers rise like breath of night,
In celestial realms, pure and bright.

The moonlight threads through branches bare,
To weave a spell, a breath of air.
Each glimmer holds a secret deep,
Where ancient spirits vigil keep.

In twilight's hush, the stories bloom,
With echoing calls that chase the gloom.
For in the dark, a spark ignites,
And guides the lost through endless nights.

The stars align, a cosmic play,
As hopes take flight, then drift away.
Yet in this dance, both grand and small,
The universe responds to all.

So heed the call, and seek your truth,
For in the dark lies hidden youth.
Beneath the roost, where dreams take flight,
The celestial sings through endless night.

Epics of the Celestial Night

Beneath the stars that softly gleam,
Where dreams entwine like silver seams,
Adventures wait in shadows cast,
In whispers of the night so vast.

The moon a lantern, shining bright,
Guides lost souls through the velvet night,
With tales of ages long since past,
And echoes of our hopes held fast.

Each comet's trail, a spark of fate,
Through cosmic realms, we navigate,
A dance of time, a stellar flight,
The epics born of celestial light.

Constellations, maps of lore,
Unravel truths we can't ignore,
In every twinkle, secrets hide,
The universe, our timeless guide.

So gather 'round, let stories weave,
In cosmic threads, we shall believe,
For as we gaze, our spirits soar,
In epics found on night's vast shore.

Tales of Enigma and Wonder

In realms where mysteries entwine,
A tapestry of fate's design,
Each whisper holds a secret key,
Unlocking worlds we long to see.

From shadows deep to light's embrace,
With every glance, a fleeting trace,
The hidden paths, the coded lines,
Where truth and fantasy combines.

A riddle sung by ancient trees,
The rustling leaves a gentle tease,
Each moment filled with breathless awe,
In every glance, the world is raw.

Through time's embrace, the wonders call,
In curious hearts, we rise and fall,
With every step, the quests arise,
In enigma, the answer lies.

So venture forth, let tales unfold,
In stories new and legends old,
With wonder as our guiding star,
We'll journey far, and never far.

The Silence of Ancient Roars

In echoes deep of time's great past,
Where shadows linger, memories cast,
The silence holds a thunderous might,
Of ancient roars in the fading light.

Mountains stand with secrets veiled,
In whispers of the winds that sailed,
Each stone a witness to the fight,
Of beasts that roamed in primal night.

The earth remembers all that's lost,
Each creak and crack a heavy cost,
Yet beauty blooms where wild things roamed,
In silence, the history's homed.

Nature's canvas, vast and grand,
In every grain of ancient sand,
The stories of the fierce and bold,
In silence, their legends unfold.

So heed the quiet, feel the lore,
For in stillness, there's much more,
As shadows dance and echoes pause,
We find the strength in ancient roars.

Secrets of the Winged Wanderers

Above the clouds, where eagles soar,
In heights unknown, we dare explore,
With wings like dreams that touch the skies,
The secrets held in each bird's eyes.

From tiny sparrows, swift and spry,
To mighty hawks that rule the high,
Each feathered soul a tale profound,
In silent flight, their truths are found.

The winds carry whispers of their flight,
Across the valleys, through the night,
With every beat, a story flies,
Of journeys long and daring highs.

In every nest, a fragile thread,
Of love and hope, where dreams are fed,
The wanderers unite and part,
In secrets held within their heart.

So let us learn from those who glide,
In worlds above where wonders bide,
For every flight beneath the sun,
Reveals the paths where we are one.

Beyond the Horizon of Lost Dreams

Where whispers of forgotten tales fly,
A glimmering light meets the twilight sky.
Each shadow dances on a sighing breeze,
Unraveling secrets hiding in the trees.

Beneath the stars, a world sleeps in gloom,
Faithful echoes chase away the doom.
Promises linger like the morning dew,
As hope renews, colors break through blue.

A distant lighthouse guides the restless soul,
Waves of nostalgia playing their role.
Carried onward by the moon's sweet song,
In the heart of night, where dreams belong.

On paths untrodden, brave spirits roam,
In search of solace, a place called home.
With each step taken, a memory blooms,
In the quiet night, where laughter looms.

So journey forth, let courage be your steed,
Past boundaries of fear, embrace the need.
For beyond the horizon, you shall find,
The treasures of dreams left far behind.

A Dance with the Winged Phantom

In the stillness, shadows began to sway,
A phantom danced in the moon's soft play.
Gossamer wings caught the silver light,
As dreams took flight in the velvety night.

Tickling the fabrics of time's endless fold,
A ballet of whispers, gentle yet bold.
With every pirouette, the world stirs awake,
A fleeting moment, a breath it can take.

Through tangled woods where no footprints lie,
Mysteries linger, breathing a sigh.
The phantom beckons with a beckoned glance,
Inviting hearts to join in the dance.

Each twirl and dip, secrets left untold,
In the arms of night, energies unfold.
With laughter echoing through the darkened pines,
The magic between us, bound by ethereal lines.

So embrace the shadows, let your spirit roam,
Amongst the wonders that call you home.
For in this dance lies a heartbeat's dream,
A waltz with the phantom, forever a theme.

Musing Upon the Celestial Stories

High above where the star-threads weave,
Silent tales are spun, hard to believe.
Legends drip from constellations' grace,
Each sparkling gem holds a secret place.

Captured glimmers of time's gentle song,
In starlit pages where the brave belong.
Echoes of stardust, woven in fate,
Callings of destiny that never abate.

Beyond the veils of reality's bounds,
Whispers of wisdom in the cosmos resound.
Galaxies swirl in an endless embrace,
In the timeless dance of the great and base.

Come hear the stories, let mind take flight,
Through the tapestry spun of shadow and light.
With every gaze up, a story unfolds,
In the heart of the night, where magic beholds.

Let each reflection inspire your own quest,
In the vastness of dreams, may you find rest.
For musing upon these celestial sights,
Will kindle the spark of your own starry nights.

The Veiled Journey of the Mystic Creature

Underneath the cloak of midnight's grace,
A mystic creature begins its chase.
With eyes like lanterns, aglow with dreams,
It glides through shadows, silent as streams.

Each furrowed path tells a tale of old,
Of ancient magic in whispers bold.
Through moonlit glades, it weaves and spins,
Carrying the weight of forgotten sins.

The air is fragrant with promise anew,
As stars cast their light, painting skies blue.
Its journey unfurls like a ribbon of mist,
Drawing in seekers who long to exist.

A guardian of tales, hidden from view,
Bestowing the brave a chance to renew.
In the depths of twilight, the creature leads,
A dance of the night where the heart truly bleeds.

So follow the wisps, let the night unfold,
As beauty embraces the brave and the bold.
For veiled journeys await in the realms of dream,
Where magic persists in a shimmering gleam.

A Journey Through Legendary Realms

In the forest deep where whispers sigh,
Ancient magic stirs and dances high.
A map unfolds with secrets vast,
As shadows flicker, the die is cast.

Through mountains steep and valleys wide,
Where forgotten spirits choose to bide.
With every step, new legends bloom,
As time unwinds in the twilight gloom.

By rivers singing of tales untold,
Heroes rise, and the brave are bold.
In the land where dreams walk free,
Adventure beckons, come wander with me.

Through portals bright to lands unknown,
With every heartbeat, courage has grown.
Together we'll chase the stories old,
In this realm where wonders unfold.

So take my hand, let our quest begin,
With hearts of lion, we shall not thin.
In legendary realms, we'll weave our fate,
For every moment, let's celebrate.

Silk and Stone: A Talisman's Tale

Beneath the moon's soft silver light,
A talisman glows, both haunting and bright.
Threads of silk and whispers of stone,
An ancient power weaves its own throne.

In a marketplace of echoes and dreams,
Where shadows dance and nothing is as it seems.
A merchant smiles, his secrets kept,
While through the night, the heart has leapt.

With every binding, a story unfolds,
Of love and loss, of ages old.
In the clasp of fate, our lives entwine,
For what is promised, in time will shine.

So journey with me through the twisting lanes,
Where magic thrives and hope remains.
With every step, the silence breaks,
As destiny stirs, the talisman wakes.

Together we'll brave the unknown night,
In a tapestry woven with dreams and light.
Through silk and stone, our spirits soar,
In tales of wonder forevermore.

Beyond the Searing Sun

When daylight fades and shadows creep,
The world transforms, in silence deep.
Beneath the skies of fiery hues,
A pathway glimmers, yours to choose.

Through scorching sands, the journey calls,
The mountains echo as darkness falls.
With courage kindled in hearts entwined,
Beyond the sun, new worlds we'll find.

A caravan whispers its age-old lore,
Of heroes past and battles bore.
In the dance of starlight, secrets gleam,
As night unveils the surface of a dream.

With hope as our guide, we press ahead,
Where ancient thirst and hunger wed.
In quiet undertones, the night does sing,
Of promises made and the joy they bring.

So greet the dawn with souls ablaze,
For every step, a new-found praise.
Beyond the searing sun, we roam,
In lands of wonder, we find our home.

The Flight of Echoing Dreams

In a world of whispers where silence flies,
Echoing dreams weave through the skies.
A flight of fancy, a heartbeat's race,
In the twilight's shimmer, we find our place.

With wings of starlight, we dare to soar,
Through valleys of shadow, we explore.
Each flutter beckons the night to play,
As horizons stretch, in shades of gray.

Beneath the canopy of our desires,
The echoes harmonize like gentle choirs.
With every breath, the mysteries call,
As we rise together, never to fall.

In the embrace of heavens wide,
Our dreams take flight, no need to hide.
For in the air where wishes gleam,
We find forever in each shared dream.

So chase the dawn, let spirits gleam,
In the dance of light, we live our dream.
The flight of echoing dreams shall last,
As we weave the future, forgetting the past.

An Invitation to the Feathered Realms

In twilight's gentle, golden glow,
The feathered friends take flight and soar,
With whispers soft and secrets low,
They beckon us to seek for more.

Through groves where wildflowers bloom bright,
And rivers sing a sweet refrain,
Their melodies fill the soft night,
Inviting hearts to share their pain.

A dance of wings in silken air,
Each flutter holds a tale untold,
We listen close, our spirits bare,
In dreams where magic we behold.

With every chirp and every call,
The world transforms beneath the moon,
In feathered realms, we stand enthralled,
Our hearts attuned to nature's tune.

So take my hand, let us explore,
The secrets held by night and sky,
In whispered songs, we'll find the core,
Of life's sweet truths that flutter by.

The Legend's Breath on the Breeze

Upon the winds, a tale unwinds,
Of heroes bold and battles won,
Each breath a spark, in memory binds,
The essence of a long-lost sun.

The whispered tales of days gone past,
Float softly through the autumn trees,
Legends rise, their shadows cast,
Like echoes carried on the breeze.

In faded tomes where dreams reside,
The chronicles of passion burn,
Each legend holds a truth, our guide,
That calls us forth, and bids return.

With every gust, the stories weave,
A tapestry of hopes and fears,
For those who listen, hearts believe,
In whispered words through fleeting years.

So let the winds our voices raise,
To honor all who came before,
In every breath, we share their praise,
As legends breathe from shore to shore.

The Whispering Stars' Call

When night unfolds her velvet cloak,
The stars ignite with silver light,
In their soft glow, the cosmos spoke,
An invitation to the night.

They twinkle with a knowing grace,
Each gleam a wish upon the dark,
In vast expanse, we find our place,
As dreams take flight, ignite a spark.

With every twirl, the heavens sigh,
A melody through time and space,
Their whispers curl like smoke to fly,
As fate entwines in endless chase.

So look up high, dear wanderer's heart,
And let the stars your journey steer,
For in their light, we find the art,
Of love and hope, of dreams held dear.

In shadows deep, where wishes pool,
The universe, a guiding call,
With every star, a cosmic jewel,
Awaits the brave to heed their thrall.

From the Heights of Ancient Echoes

From mountain tops where silence reigns,
The weight of years drips like the dew,
With echoes loud, the history gains,
A symphony of time anew.

The stones have stories, etched in time,
Their whispers told through rustling leaves,
In shadows deep, we seek to climb,
To hear the secrets silence weaves.

Each step unveils a world unknown,
Where once the ancients walked and spoke,
Through silent paths and walls of stone,
The past entwines with every joke.

So let us wander, hand in hand,
To heights where dreams and echoes play,
Together, we will understand,
The wisdom found in yesterday.

For in those heights, we'll breathe once more,
The tales of time that shape our fate,
With every echo, we restore,
The lost connections we create.

The Call of the Winged Seers

In shadows cast by moon's tender light,
The winged seers soar, silent and bright.
Their whispers flutter with tales of yore,
Secrets of magic reside evermore.

With feathers like ink, they sketch the night,
Drawing dreams on clouds, a wondrous sight.
They beckon the brave, those lost to despair,
With promises woven in the cool, crisp air.

In twilight's embrace, they gather at dawn,
Each heart a canvas, together they're drawn.
The song of the skies, a haunting refrain,
Calls forth the lost, as they dance through the rain.

Through forests of starlight, their visions convey,
Stories of hope in the light of the day.
And near the rivers where dreams intertwine,
The call of the winged seers softly aligns.

Notes from the Tunisian Sky

Beneath the sun, where the desert winds blow,
The Tunisian sky holds secrets in tow.
Stars scatter like whispers, precious and rare,
Illuminating pathways devoid of despair.

Among the dunes where the silences sleep,
A symphony echoes, both delicate and deep.
The colors of twilight wrap all in their grace,
Painting the heavens, a warm, tender embrace.

In the stillness of night, the stories unfold,
Of ancients and treasures, of legends retold.
The moon stands as witness to every sweet sigh,
As dreams take their flight across the vast sky.

With each passing hour, the stars seem to wink,
Guiding lost travelers, urging them to think.
In Tunisia's cradle where the wild roses grow,
The notes of the sky wrap the world in their glow.

A Reverie of Feathers and Folklore

In a world spun of magic, where whispers reside,
Feathers drift lightly, on breezes they glide.
Folklore surrounds them, like shadows at play,
Carrying tales from the ancients far away.

Each plume tells a story, of love and of loss,
Of gallant adventure, of fortunes that cross.
The dance of the crows sings in echoes so bold,
While dreams ride the currents of secrets untold.

From the depths of the woods, where the echoes align,
To realms where the stars weave their magical line.
The whispers of ages are caught on the wing,
As legends awaken, and soft visions sing.

In a reverie deep, when the night paints its guise,
Feathers and folklore entwine in the skies.
Together they twinkle, like gems on a thread,
A tapestry woven, where imagination is fed.

The Luminous Secrets of the Sky

In the canvas of dusk, where wonders unfold,
The sky tells its secrets in colors of gold.
With a shimmer of starlight that dances and gleams,
The luminous truths are spun from our dreams.

As twilight descends, shadows stretch long,
A chorus of constellations sings their sweet song.
The whispers of astral winds beckon us near,
Holding our hearts with a gentle good cheer.

In silence, we ponder the stories they share,
Of comets and wishes that linger in air.
Each twinkle a promise, each flicker a fate,
Underneath all the wonders, the universe waits.

So gaze at the heavens, let your spirit take flight,
The luminous secrets around you ignite.
For in that vastness, where dreams intertwine,
The magic of the sky is forever divine.

Tales from the Realm of Skyward Wonders

In realms where skies meet dreams so high,
A whisper floats where the larks do fly,
Cloud castles gleam with tales untold,
Of daring knights and hearts so bold.

On silver wings, the legends soar,
Past azure waves on a golden shore,
The realms unfold with each gentle breeze,
As hope and magic dance in the trees.

Stars twinkle bright in the velvet night,
Guiding souls who seek the light,
With every heartbeat, the stories weave,
In the tapestry of dreams that we believe.

From ancient scripts to the skies aglow,
The tales arise where the wild winds blow,
A saga sung by spirits of lore,
Where wonder waits on every shore.

So listen closely, dear hearts awake,
In every shadow, a wish to make,
For in the realm of wonders so wide,
Adventure calls on the winds of pride.

A Tapestry of Feathers and Legends

In quiet glades where secrets dwell,
The tapestry of time weaves stories well,
Feathers drift like whispers divine,
Crafting legends on the edges of time.

Golden beaks and wings that flare,
Dancing through the scented air,
Each flutter holds a secret's grace,
In this enchanted, timeless place.

The ancients speak through rustling leaves,
Tales of quests and hearts that believe,
Looming shadows in twilight hue,
Guide the brave who seek what's true.

In every feather, a story sings,
Of mighty quests and celestial beings,
Binding dreams in the moonlight's hue,
With every tale, a world anew.

So gather round, let spirits soar,
A tapestry woven forevermore,
Lend your ear to the magic at play,
In the dance of feathers that light the way.

The Lament of the Winged Shadows

In twilight's grasp, the shadows creep,
Where silent wings in dark do weep,
A haunting song fills the starry air,
Of forgotten dreams and lost despair.

Once, they soared on winds of grace,
Chasing the dawn, a swift embrace,
Now they linger, a mournful tune,
Beneath the watchful, silver moon.

Their echoes dance in the still of night,
Wings once radiant, now void of light,
The stories told through sighs and cries,
As time slips past in forlorn skies.

Each shadow holds a tale of yore,
Of battles fought and hearts that bore,
A lament spun like threads of fate,
In whispers soft, they resonate.

So heed their call, the winged away,
For in their sorrow lies truth's ray,
A journey lost in the passage of years,
The echoes linger, the silent tears.

Voyage of the Mythic Beasts

On oceans vast where legends drift,
Mythic beasts on adventures lift,
With eyes aglow and hearts so strong,
They sail the skies, where dreams belong.

Dragons weave through clouds like lace,
In search of realms, an unknown place,
With every roar, a story ignites,
As stars awaken in mystical nights.

The phoenix flames on wings of gold,
In fiery dance, their tale unfolds,
From ashes rise, with courage anew,
A testament to what dreams can do.

Griffins soar with a regal flair,
Guardians of treasures, they shun despair,
Guiding lost souls to places bright,
In the wonder of day and the cloak of night.

With every legend, a map is drawn,
To worlds unseen before the dawn,
Join the voyage, let your spirit fly,
On mythical wings, through endless sky.

Reflections on the Edge of Night

Whispers creep as shadows play,
The moonlight weaves a silver fray.
Thoughts drift like clouds in a velvet sky,
While stars converse in a silent sigh.

Secrets stir in the cool night air,
Each flickering flame holds a silent prayer.
Time slows down as dreams take flight,
In the tender embrace of the coming night.

Echoes call from places unknown,
Where wishes and fears have softly grown.
The heart remembers what the mind can't seek,
In the quiet hour, it dares to speak.

Glimmers dance on the edge of sleep,
While the world outside begins to weep.
Voices fade, yet still they linger,
As hope is cradled on a gentle finger.

So let the twilight wrap you tight,
In the shadows that slip from sight.
For in each moment lies a chance,
To find your soul in the nighttime dance.

The Silent Choir of the Winds

Amidst the trees, the breezes sigh,
Nature's chorus, a lullaby.
Invisible fingers strum the leaves,
Each note a secret that nature weaves.

Whispers soft as the moon's embrace,
A symphony born from time and space.
In the rustling grass, a gentle tune,
Carried along by the light of the moon.

Winds shall speak in a thousand ways,
Of sunlit glades and misty bays.
They carry tales of deep, secret worlds,
Where magic breathes and wonder unfurls.

Listen close to their melodic cries,
For in their music, a truth lies.
A harmony sung to the lost and found,
In the quiet hymn of the earth's profound.

So let the winds guide your weary hearts,
With whispers of hope as the daylight departs.
For in their song, we find our peace,
An everlasting echo that will never cease.

Songs of the Four Winds

North wind howls with icy breath,
Bearing tales of life and death.
It stirs the soul with a chilling grace,
Like a ghostly echo, a fleeting trace.

East wind dances with the dawn,
Bringing warmth as the night is drawn.
With golden light, it sweeps the day,
Painting dreams in a vibrant display.

Southern breezes whisper sweet,
Soft and gentle, a lover's greet.
They caress the world with a tender touch,
Sowing seeds of courage and such.

West wind carries the scent of rain,
Cleansing hearts from sorrow and pain.
It sings of change with a calming sound,
As hope and renewal together are found.

Together they weave a tapestry rare,
In every gust, in every stare.
The songs of the winds, a timeless flight,
Guiding us home through the shadows of night.

The Alchemy of Dreams and Feathers

In the stillness of night, dreams take form,
Turning whispers of thoughts into a storm.
Feathers drift on the edge of sleep,
Carrying tales that the shadows keep.

Alchemy brews in the depths of mind,
Binding the past, future intertwined.
With each flutter, a story unfurls,
Crafting magic in a world of pearls.

As stars emerge, dreams ignite the air,
Filling the void where silence dares.
A dance of the heart, a flicker of grace,
In the alchemy found in this sacred space.

Hearts collide with the essence of night,
Transforming darkness into radiant light.
Every feather's trail, a spark of gold,
Whispering secrets of life untold.

So let your spirit take flight and soar,
In the alchemy of dreams, forever explore.
For in the weave of the night's embrace,
Lies the magic of time and space.

Guardians of the Hidden Realm

In cloaks of dusk, they silently tread,
With whispers of magic, softly spread.
From shadows they watch, with eyes aglow,
The guardians of secrets in the trees below.

They weave through the twilight, a dance so rare,
In the depths of the forest, a bond to share.
Keeping the balance of life and fate,
These silent watchers, our world's soul-mates.

With ancient wisdom, they guide the lost,
Through trials and journeys, no matter the cost.
Their laughter rings clear like the bell's gentle chime,
Echoing truths in the fabric of time.

So when the night falls, and dreams take flight,
Remember the guardians that guard the night.
For in their embrace, we are never alone,
In the realm of the hidden, we find our home.

The Journey of the Feathered Giants

High aloft on wings of might,
The feathered giants take their flight.
With a cry that echoes through the skies,
Over mountains, beneath sunrises.

They sail on winds both fierce and free,
Chasing horizons, where none can see.
Guided by stars in the velvet night,
Their path unknown, yet always bright.

Through storms they soar, unbound by fear,
Drifting through clouds, drawing near.
With each new dawn, the journey unfolds,
In silence, their ancient story is told.

Clad in plumage of golden hue,
The guardians of skies, brave and true.
In awe we watch, as they round the bend,
These giants of feather, on whom we depend.

Chronicles of Dreaming Skies

In the twilight hour, where dreams take flight,
The chronicles start, in the velvet night.
Stars weave stories 'cross the vast domain,
In whispers of starlight, joy and pain.

Each twinkling gem a secret untold,
A tale of adventure, both brave and bold.
The moon, a sentinel, watches with care,
As fantasies swirl in the cool night air.

Winds carry echoes of laughter and tears,
Spanning the ages, through countless years.
The tapestry glimmers with hopes anew,
In realms of dreaming, where wishes come true.

From dusk's embrace, till dawn's first light,
The chronicles linger, a perennial sight.
So close your eyes, and let them unfold,
The magic of dreaming, forever retold.

Beneath the Arcane Starry Canopy

Under the canopy of an endless sky,
Whispers of wonders from ages gone by.
Here magic lingers in the cool night air,
Beneath the stars, we are free from care.

The constellations weave tales in the dark,
Guiding lost travelers toward their spark.
Each twinkle a promise, a wish cast wide,
In this sacred space where the heart can confide.

With every breeze, an enchantment flows,
Mysterious tunes that only night knows.
The moonlight dances on leaves with grace,
A gentle reminder of our rightful place.

So when shadows fall, and we glance above,
Remember the magic, the light, and love.
For beneath the arcane, the starlight's glow,
Lies a world of wonder, waiting to show.

Folklore of the Veiled Summit

In shadows deep where whispers dwell,
Old tales of magic weave their spell.
A mountain high, with secrets old,
Guarded by beasts both fierce and bold.

The fog rolls thick, a shroud of night,
As stars above begin their flight.
A flicker of hope in the darkened skies,
Where dreams take flight and courage lies.

With each brave step upon the stone,
The heart beats loud, no longer alone.
For those who seek the hidden truth,
May find a spark of eternal youth.

The winds will tell of love and loss,
Of heroes bold and the paths they cross.
In every crevice lies a song,
Of ancient voices, forever strong.

So gather near, and hearken well,
To tales of old that cast a spell.
For at the summit, magic stirs,
In the midnight dance of whispered furs.

Echoes of Lost Enchantment

Beneath the boughs of ancient trees,
Whispers flutter on the breeze.
A melody of days gone by,
Where laughter fades and sorrows sigh.

In every glen, the shadows play,
Their secrets dance till break of day.
Once vibrant spells now softly fade,
As time bewitches the dreams we made.

The moonlight casts a silver net,
On memories that linger yet.
In echoes soft, enchantments trace,
A fleeting glimpse of a bygone grace.

Wanderers tread on paths unknown,
For journeys led by heart alone.
In every style, the tales unfold,
Of magic lost and life retold.

Come closer now, let shadows weave,
The fabric of what we believe.
For in this realm of endless night,
Awaits the spark of lost delight.

Chronicles from the Arcane Heights

On craggy peaks where spirits soar,
The tales of magic beckon more.
A winding path through misty dreams,
Where nothing's ever as it seems.

In cloaked shadows, secrets rise,
To meet the stars in velvet skies.
Each stone a word, each breeze a sigh,
Of chronicles that never die.

Through ancient scripts, the fables flow,
Of wizards wise and tales of woe.
In wisdom's grasp, the ages bide,
With every breath, their truths collide.

Beyond the reach of time's cruel hand,
Lie histories written in the sand.
Where every tear and laughter blend,
To shape the stories without end.

So gather round as twilight falls,
And heed the ancient, timeless calls.
For in these heights, the magic lies,
In the heart of those who dare to rise.

Whims of the Celestial Guardians

In constellations bright, they dwell,
Guardians casting a shimmering spell.
With starlit laughter, they weave the night,
Guiding lost souls to morning light.

Their whims alight like shooting stars,
A dance of destiny, dreams, and scars.
Each twinkle holds a secret vast,
Of futures bright and shadows past.

When dawn breaks soft on dewy plains,
Their whispers echo through valleys' veins.
A tapestry of fate and chance,
Where every moment holds a glance.

For in the skies, their stories flow,
In cosmic ink, the tales bestow.
The quiet strength of unseen guides,
Protecting hearts where wonder hides.

So lift your gaze to heavens wide,
Embrace the magic they provide.
For those who dream beneath the stars,
Shall dance with timeless, guiding scars.

Whispers of the Celestial Beasts

In moonlit glades where shadows play,
The ancient beasts of night drift by,
With eyes like stars that guide the way,
They share their secrets, soft and spry.

A rustle here, a sigh so deep,
Their whispers blend with the night's soft tune,
While dreams awaken from their sleep,
Under the watchful gaze of the moon.

Each creature holds a tale untold,
In the silence where the spirits dwell,
Of distant lands and treasures bold,
They weave their stories, cast a spell.

Beneath the branches, shadows leap,
With every flicker, worlds collide,
In twilight hours, their yarns weep,
A mystical dance, a gentle guide.

So close your eyes, and breathe them in,
The whispers call from realms unknown,
Where celestial beasts, their tales begin,
In every heart, their magic's sown.

Echoes from the Feathered Peaks

High above where eagles soar,
The feathered winds begin to sing,
In lofty heights, they seek and tour,
Each echo carries tales of spring.

Their wings paint stories in the air,
With every flap, a new refrain,
The mountain breeze, a tender care,
Whispers secrets of joy and pain.

Among the cliffs, where shadows hide,
The echoes mingle, bright and clear,
A chorus born of nature's pride,
Resounding strong for all to hear.

While twilight drapes the peaks in gold,
The birds unite in twilight song,
A testament to dreams retold,
In every note, they all belong.

So listen close to skies above,
The feathered peaks, they hold the key,
In every sound, a hint of love,
The echoes set our spirits free.

Legends Beneath the Twilight Sky

Beneath the veil of twilight's hue,
Legends linger, soft and bright,
Whispers of realms where dreams come true,
A tapestry woven in the night.

Each star a tale, each flickering light,
Guides lost wanderers to their fate,
In shimmering hues of dark and white,
They hold the key to open gates.

Ancient voices beckon from afar,
With every breeze, the stories flow,
A dance of shadows, a guiding star,
In the twilight's fold, the magic grows.

From the depths of time, they call our name,
These legends breathe in the starry gloom,
Awake our hearts with eternal flame,
In every echo, the night will bloom.

So stand beneath this sky so wide,
Embrace the tales, let spirit soar,
With every whisper, find your guide,
In legends lost, discover more.

Chronicles of the Winged Sentinel

In the heart of the storm, a sentinel flies,
With wings outstretched against the gray,
Guardian of dreams, beneath swirling skies,
He watches over night and day.

With every flap, he stirs the air,
A silent vow, a promise made,
Through the shadows, his watchful stare,
In every storm, he won't be swayed.

The spirit of ages dwells in his flight,
A tale of valor in soft embrace,
He gathers whispers from the night,
With grace entwined, he claims his space.

From mountain high to valley low,
The chronicles of time unfold,
A dance of fate, a subtle flow,
In every feather, legends bold.

So let his story echo far,
In hearts awakened by his call,
For in the night, you'll find a star,
The winged sentinel watches all.

The Forgotten Saga of the Feathered Giants

Once in a realm where shadows danced,
Feathered giants soared in a trance.
Their wings painted skies in vibrant hue,
Ancient whispers, secrets they knew.

In valleys deep where echoes play,
Legends woven in twilight's sway.
Their calls resonated, a haunting hymn,
A past forgotten, memories dim.

Through leaves of gold, their shadows cast,
A tale of courage, shadowed by the past.
For in their flight, hope dared to rise,
Beyond the borders of earthly ties.

As storms brewed fierce, they took to air,
Guardians of dreams, beyond compare.
In twilight's glow, their spirits entwined,
A saga eternal, by fate designed.

But time is fickle, and silence fell,
The feathered giants, a distant bell.
Yet in the hearts of those who believe,
Their legacy lives, forever to weave.

Revelations from the Celestial Pillars

Upon the pillars, stars alight,
Whispers of majesty, shimmering bright.
Each glimmering tale, a beacon of hope,
Guiding lost souls like a celestial rope.

Secrets of ages swirl in the air,
Fates intertwined, burdens to bear.
From dusk till dawn, the heavens sigh,
In their embrace, dreams flutter and fly.

Through cosmic winds, the echoes unfurl,
Knowledge ancient in a twinkling swirl.
With each revelation, the heart takes flight,
Illuminating shadows, igniting the night.

The pillars stand tall, guardians of lore,
Holding the past, the future's door.
Ancient voices reverberate clear,
Through the fabric of time, they draw near.

In the quiet moments when stars align,
The mysteries of life in harmony shine.
For every whisper from the skies above,
Is a testament of courage, hope, and love.

The Longing of the Winged Sages

In realms unseen, where silence breathes,
Winged sages search through autumn leaves.
With eyes of wisdom, they roam the skies,
In pursuit of the truth, where the heart lies.

Through the veils of mist, their echoes call,
Guardians of dreams, they shall not fall.
In the dance of shadows, they find their grace,
Longing for knowledge in time and space.

Each feathered flutter ignites the night,
Kindling the fire with soft starlight.
Bound by the whispers from ages gone,
They seek the path where fate moves on.

With every dawn, a journey begins,
In the tapestry of life, it spins.
For in their longing, a promise glows,
An adventure awaits where the wind blows.

And so they soar on wings of lore,
Searching for treasures on yonder shore.
In the heart of the cosmos, they find their place,
A timeless pursuit, a celestial chase.

Through the Lenses of Mythic Lore

Through lenses crafted from the past,
Mythic tales in shadows cast.
Each story whispers, each legend sings,
Of ancient battles and mighty kings.

In forgotten scrolls, the truth unfurls,
A tapestry woven of worlds and pearls.
From realms of magic and dreams untold,
The echoes of wisdom begin to unfold.

Through the lens of time, we glimpse the light,
A journey through darkness, forging our fight.
For every tale holds a lesson deep,
In the heart of the night, where shadows creep.

With every page turned, a spark ignites,
Igniting passion for wondrous sights.
Mythic lore, a compass for the soul,
Guiding lost seekers towards their goal.

So let us wander through these tales so grand,
In the kingdom of words, let us take a stand.
For through the lenses, our spirits shall soar,
Awakening magic, forevermore.

Tales of the Ancient Talon

In the forest where whispers sigh,
A talon rests, 'neath the twilight sky.
Ancient stories etched in stone,
Guarding secrets in a world unknown.

Winds carry tales of the bold and brave,
Of whispers lost in the echoing cave.
The shadows dance 'round the old oak's heart,
As the spirits awaken and play their part.

A feather falls, kissed by the night,
Bringing luck, a sign of light.
With magic woven through the air,
The talon's strength shall always share.

Through the thicket, the brave ones stride,
With courage as their trusted guide.
In the realm where enchantments blend,
The talon's tale shall never end.

Shadows of the Stellar Roar

Under a blanket of shimmering stars,
The universe sings of distant wars.
Echoes whisper from the far-off past,
Of journeys taken, shadows cast.

Moonlight dances on the silver lake,
While dreams awaken, and hearts shall ache.
The stellar roar calls from above,
A symphony of tales, wrapped in love.

Constellations tell of battles won,
Of heroes risen with the morning sun.
Each twinkle a promise, a hope anew,
Spinning stories, forever true.

In the silence, secrets hide,
Waiting for hearts open wide.
Courage whispers from the cosmic shore,
Inviting all to seek for more.

Fables of the Mystic Talon

By the stream where the moonlight gleams,
Lives a talon woven with dreams.
From dusk till dawn, it flies so high,
Carrying tales 'neath the velvet sky.

Fables born of earth and sky,
Whispers of wonders that never die.
Each feather tells of a daring flight,
Illuminating shadows with purest light.

In the twilight, shadows play,
As the talon glides through night and day.
With every beat, its magic flows,
Guiding lost wanderers where love grows.

Through valleys deep and mountains steep,
The mystic talon wakes from sleep.
Carving paths through realms unknown,
Its ancient wisdom shall be shown.

Secrets of the Enchanted Ridge

Atop the ridge where silence reigns,
Lie secrets hidden, wrapped in chains.
The winds blow softly, secrets spill,
Echoes dance to the mountains' thrill.

Luminous paths of shimmering light,
Guide the dreamers through the night.
Ancient stones guard tales of yore,
Inviting others to seek and explore.

A talon clutches the keys to time,
Unlocking fables, entwined in rhyme.
Whispers call from the depths of stone,
Awakening dreams once thought alone.

Through mist and magic, destiny weaves,
Tales of courage hidden in leaves.
On the enchanted ridge, we find the grace,
Of a secret world, a timeless space.

Beneath the Veil of Celestial Wonders

Beneath the veil of stars so bright,
A tapestry of dreams takes flight,
With whispers soft from worlds unseen,
In magic spun, where hearts convene.

The moonlight weaves a silken thread,
Upon the waves where wishes spread,
A dance of light on shadowed seas,
Where wonders bathe in midnight breeze.

Each flicker tells a tale profound,
Of ancient lore in silence found,
As constellations guide our way,
Unraveling mysteries at play.

In twilight's glow, our hopes ignite,
With every breath, we chase the night,
Exploring realms where stardust lies,
And dreams ascend to endless skies.

So let us wander, hearts aglow,
Through cosmic paths, where spirits flow,
Beneath the veil of night's embrace,
We seek our truths in endless space.

Reflections on Azure Wings

Upon the winds of azure skies,
Bright wings take flight with whispered sighs,
In shadows cast by sunlit gleam,
They dance entwined in nature's dream.

With every flutter, tales arise,
Of journeys wild and love's disguise,
As colors blend in softest hues,
Awakening the heart anew.

The breeze will carry secrets sweet,
Of laughter shared and hopes we meet,
In every rise and gentle fall,
The magic beckons, calls us all.

Through stormy skies and sunbeams bright,
Reflections shimmer, pure delight,
A reminder in our fleeting days,
That beauty's found in myriad ways.

So let us soar on azure wings,
To realms where freedom's spirit sings,
In every whisper, every glance,
We find our joy in life's sweet dance.

Legends from the Echoing Heights

In mountains high where legends breathe,
The winds carry tales of those who seethe,
With hopes and dreams like eagles soar,
Through valleys deep and ancient lore.

Each stone a witness, every tree,
Holds echoes of our history,
In twilight's glow, their stories bloom,
Like flowers bursting from the gloom.

The sky is painted with their cries,
As spirits ride the dusk-lit skies,
With every shadow, shadows weave,
The paths of yore we still believe.

Through whispered winds, they guide our fate,
With wisdom forged through love and weight,
Their voices blend with nature's call,
A symphony that binds us all.

So listen close to echoes grand,
For legends rise and take their stand,
In echoing heights where dreams entwine,
Our hearts united, spirit divine.

The Enigma of the Silver Plume

In twilight's glow, a plume unfurls,
As mysteries weave through somber swirls,
A silver thread in shadows cast,
A glimpse of futures, echoes past.

What secrets lie within its guise?
Each feathered whisper, soft surprise,
A call to venture, bold and free,
To follow dreams where hearts decree.

With every flutter, shadows dance,
Enticing souls to take a chance,
To seek the path, though veiled in night,
Illuminated by hope's pure light.

The enigma rests on a gentle breeze,
In every sigh, the heart's unease,
Yet courage blooms where doubts reside,
And silken wings become our guide.

So let us chase the silver plume,
Embrace the whispers, banish gloom,
For in the quest, we find our song,
In sweet adventure, we belong.

Between the Clouds and Shadows

In whispers soft, the breezes flow,
Where sunlight dances, and shadows grow.
Above the world, so vast and high,
The dreams of wanderers softly lie.

A tapestry of azure seas,
Where hopes are carried on the breeze.
Each cloud a vessel of the heart,
In skies where sorrows drift apart.

With silver threads, the twilight weaves,
A story of the heart that believes.
Where light and shadow waltz and twine,
In this realm, the stars align.

As nightfall whispers, secrets spun,
The dance of day is almost done.
Yet in the dark, new worlds arise,
In every drop of moonlit skies.

So lift your gaze to heights untold,
Embrace the mysteries of the bold.
Between the clouds, let your heart soar,
To realms unseen, forevermore.

The Winged Watchers' Lament

Above the trees, the winged grace,
They sail the winds, they find their place.
With feathers bright, they seek the dawn,
Yet linger still, 'til daylight's gone.

In solemn flight, they guard the skies,
With watchful gaze, they ever rise.
Each cry a song of ancient lore,
In silence held, they're evermore.

From heights profound, their spirits soar,
In twilight hues, they seek for more.
What dreams do drift, what tales are spun,
For those who glide 'til day is done?

Yet as they fly, the world looks on,
For every dusk must greet the dawn.
Their wings, a tapestry of fate,
In sorrow's depths, they patiently wait.

Oh winged watchers, in skies so wide,
Your silent strength, a trusty guide.
In harmony, your wings will sing,
And through the night, hope takes to wing.

Whispers from the Forgotten Cliffs

On craggy heights, the secrets dwell,
In echoes of a whispered spell.
The cliffs, they guard the tales of yore,
Of love and loss, forevermore.

The ocean's sigh, a gentle breeze,
As twilight casts its mystic tease.
Each stone a memory, old yet new,
Crafted by tides that always knew.

From fissures deep, the stories rise,
Of spirits bound to earth and skies.
In quiet tones, they call to those,
Who dare to listen where the wind blows.

Amidst the mist, the shadows dance,
A fleeting glimpse, a cherished chance.
In every heart, the whispers stay,
Reminders of the light of day.

As night enfolds the cliffs so grand,
The spirits reach for hand in hand.
In every breath of salty air,
The echoes linger, everywhere.

Secrets Entwined in Feather and Flame

In twilight's grip, where shadows gleam,
A dance of secrets, a whispered dream.
Feathers drift on the breath of night,
Tales of fire, and of flight.

With ember glow, the memories spark,
In hearts that blaze against the dark.
Each flicker holds a story's way,
In hopes that guide the night to day.

The winds they carry the lost refrain,
Of whispered joys and muted pain.
Voices entwined in the smoky air,
In every flicker, they lay bare.

As dawn approaches with gentle grace,
The secrets find their rightful place.
In every feather, every flame,
The essence of the world retains.

So cherish well the tales you find,
In feathered whispers, intertwined.
For in this dance of light and dark,
The heart will find its truest spark.

Echoes of Enchanted Fables

In woods where shadows softly play,
A breeze sings secrets, come what may.
The trees, they murmur tales of old,
Of magic spun and hearts so bold.

Beneath the moon's watchful gaze,
Whispers dance in the silver haze.
A flicker of hope, a flicker of light,
Guiding the lost through the dark of night.

From the brook to the stone, they flow,
Stories of dreams that ebb and grow.
With every heartbeat, time weaves around,
An orchestra of voices profound.

So gather ye round, the fireside bright,
As echoes of fables take to flight.
Each tale a ribbon, each laugh a strand,
Together we craft this wondrous land.

Tales Whispers Beyond the Horizon

Across the sea where the stars collide,
Whispers of journeys ever abide.
Where sailboats glide on a shimmering crest,
And every wave carries dreams expressed.

In the twilight's embrace, tales are spun,
Of daring adventurers who chase the sun.
With hearts aglow and spirits free,
They seek the treasures of the deep blue sea.

From the shore, a longing call does sound,
Of distant lands and magic found.
An echo that lingers in the breeze,
Where the world awakens with playful ease.

In the twilight sky where wonders bloom,
Dreams whisper softly, dispelling gloom.
So heed this call, let the tales unfurl,
And journey beyond the edge of the world.

Legends Carved in Celestial Stone

In the heart of mountains, ancient and grand,
Legends lie written in the earth's own hand.
Each crack a story, each peak a rhyme,
Whispers of ages lost in time.

Beneath the stars that twinkle with grace,
Tales of heroes and their chase.
From battlefields to love's sweet song,
In the stone, their spirits belong.

Echoes of laughter, echoes of pain,
Tales of loss that ripple like rain.
In the silence of night, they rise and swell,
Guarded by shadows where they dwell.

So wander forth, brave souls, awake!
Seek out the legends the ancients make.
Each stone a chapter, each path a thread,
Where whispers live and the heart is led.

The Feathered Beasts of Ancient Lore

Above in the skies where the legends play,
Feathered beasts soar, come what may.
With wings of fire and a heart of gold,
Each flaps a story waiting to unfold.

From the mountains to valleys so vast,
Their shadows dance, a spell is cast.
In the hush of dawn, their call rings clear,
A melody borne from yesteryear.

In swirling clouds and the winds that sigh,
We find the echoes of their cry.
A world awakened with magic's grace,
In each feather lies a sacred space.

So lift your gaze and look above,
For there, the skies breathe tales of love.
With every flap, a new dream flies,
The feathered beasts dance across our skies.

9 781805 635925